Birthday Tracker

Journal

This Tracker/Journal Belongs to:

_____

Birthday Tracker

&

Journal

*Cover art, introduction,
and illustrated with
color drawings, paintings, and collages*

Jan Yager, Ph.D.

HANNACROIX CREEK BOOKS, INC.
Stamford, Connecticut

Dedicated to my family and friends
with thanks for remembering me on my special day,
and, most of all, every day, for your love and friendship

Birthday Tracker and Journal
Published by:
Hannacroix Creek Books, Inc.
1127 High Ridge Road, #110
Stamford, Connecticut 06905 USA
http://www.hannacroixcreekbooks.com
e-mail: hannacroix@aol.com
Follow us on twitter: www.twitter.com/hannacroixcreek

ISBN: 978-1-889262-79-6 (hardcover) (13-digit)
          1-889262-79-X (hardcover) (10-digit)

ISBN: 978-1-889262-80-2 (trade paperback) (13-digit)
          1-889262-80-3 (trade paperback) (10-digit)

Interior Layout & Design by Scribe Freelance | www.scribefreelance.com

Illustrations by Jan Yager (in order of presentation)
Cover art, "Flowers in a vase," marker, wallpaper, sequins, on paper
"Happy birthday butterflies" Acrylic and plastic leaves on paper
Candle, marker on watercolor paper
Balloons, marker on watercolor paper
Red flower with yellow beads on black background
"Spring Connecticut scene" (markers and pastel on paper)
Parrot (paper collage)
Vase with flowers (Acrylic painting/collage with wallpaper)
Living room chair with photo (watercolor markers on paper)
Vase on paper drawn with marker with charcoal
"Cat in the window" (acrylic painting with plastic blinds)
Flowering plant in pot, markers, paper, and fabric
Bookshelves and sofa, line drawing
Leaf collage with linoleum block printing
Pink, yellow, and red flowers collage with sequins and shiny green leaves
Poinsettia collage with papers and marker (on card stock)
Linoleum block/collage of vase with beads and sequins
Self-portrait of the author/artist as a young woman (acrylic on board)

BIRTHDAYS AND BIRTHDAY CELEBRATIONS:
An Introduction

Your birthday. It only happens once a year, but oh how special that day is to the birthday child or adult and to his or her family and friends as well. Many of us take for granted the customs and traditions associated with birthday celebrations, but there is a history to how birthday rituals have evolved, and there are also distinct cultural differences in birthday traditions around the world.

It is believed that the first birthday parties were celebrated to keep away evil spirits that were more likely to plague someone on his or her birthday. Giving gifts was supposed to also ward off the evil spirits.

Whose birthday is more important, yours or those you care about? This philosophical question seems to have been pondered as far back as ancient Rome. In Kathyrn Argetsinger's scholarly article, "Birthday rituals: Friends and Patrons in Roman Poetry and Cult," she points out that celebrating the birthday of a friend or a patron was considered at least as significant, and possibly even more so, than noting one's own birthday.

In ancient Rome, in addition to the celebration of private birthdays, there was also the custom of celebrating the birthdays of past and present rulers. It is said that is where the tradition of the birthday boy or girl wearing a crown began.

BIRTHDAY CAKE

Some date the birthday cake to ancient Greece when a round honey cake or bread was taken to the temple of Artemis, the goddess of the moon. It is also suggested that the custom of putting candles on a birthday cake was introduced by the Greeks; candles made the offered cake glow more like the moon. But the originator of what has become the traditional birthday cake is attributed to Germany in the Middle Ages when a sweetened layer cake was used for birthday celebrations.

Birthday cakes continue to have special meaning, especially in the absence of more elaborate celebrations. As 83-year-old Floriana Hall, author of 12 books, shares: "I grew up during The Great Depression and had only one birthday party. However, our family tradition was to make a banana nut cake for all our family's birthdays. When my mother had the ingredients on our birthday, she would bake the banana cake. That was a tradition in her family for years even when her great grandparents lived in Alsace-Lorraine." This is a ritual that Floriana's continued: "I love having my family all together for each person's birthday and I bake a banana nut cake from scratch just like my mother and her mother did before her."

A colleague in Romania shared with me that during her childhood "there was a tradition that if it was your birthday, you should eat the cake from a glass without using a spoon. It was funny." But she has not heard of this tradition being recently observed.

Kathyrn Kleinman's illustrated book, *Birthday Cakes* includes 38 recipes from such cooks as James Beard and Julia Child with recipes for making a German Chocolate Cake or a Princess Cake, a Swedish sweet sixteen tradition.

BIRTHDAY PARTIES

It is also suggested that it was in Germany two hundred years ago when the practice of having birthday parties for children began. It was called *kinderfeste* (*kinder* "children" + *feste* "party"). Today, birthdays are still special for children and adults alike in Germany and around the world. A working woman in Frankfurt, Germany says, "Parents usually organize a party with family members (especially grandparents), neighbors and maybe friends from kindergarten or elementary school. This usually happens in the afternoon with the kids playing games and the grown-ups having cake (birthday cake!) and coffee, and taking plenty of pictures. Presents can be anything from toys or money for their future which is put into a savings account."

Historian Elizabeth Pleck notes in "A Brief History of Birthday parties" in the alumni magazine of University of Illinois, that during the early 1800s, in Victorian England, birthday parties offered an opportunity to demonstrate etiquette and "to teach children the manners they would need to assume their place of privilege in society." Celebrating one's birthday with friends in a lavish way is one of the perks of fame and fortune. For example, media mogul Malcolm Forbes spent $2.5 million on his 70th birthday party, which was held in Tangier, Morocco. Forbes chartered three planes to take 800 guests from New York and London to his party. Some of the guests included actress Elizabeth Taylor, former secretary of state Henry Kissinger, and many CEOs.

Whether a birthday celebration is a lavish party, costing lots of money, a gathering of a couple of friends at the local bowling alley, or a surprise party, the most important element is that someone is remembered. Of course it is best if the celebration coincides with the actual birthday. But if that is not possible — if the party is over the weekend even though the birthday is during the school or work week — on the actual birthday, there should still be a recognition of that special day.

I vividly remember my first birthday party with my peers when I was five years old. My mother asked me to invite the entire class in elementary school, which was the custom at that time, so no one would feel left out. Around twenty of my classmates assembled in the basement of my house where a table had been set up so we could have the hot dogs and beans that was served. We played "Pin the Tale on the Donkey," a popular birthday party game back in the 1950s. Since my birthday fell in December, my mother had my older brother dress up as Santa Claus and give out presents to all my classmates even though we were Jewish.

My mother had the best of intensions, but after that experience birthday parties have never been high on my list of positive celebrations although my husband Fred threw me a memorable 40th birthday party that was held in the living room of our apartment in Manhattan. (I made a very special wish over my birthday candles, and, as is the tradition and superstition, I kept the wish to myself, and the wish did come true!)

Here is what a mother shared in a blog about what happened when her daughter Tara turned five and she celebrated her birthday in India:

> 5 cakes to turn 5. Celebrating her birthday in India, my daughter, Tara has been showered with love, attention, gifts, fortune and awareness.
>
> On her birthday, Tara woke up to balloons, phone calls, and presents. She met her 4 living great grandparents. She had lunch with her four grandparents. She met her cousins. She had a tea birthday party at home with friends. My aunt, another "great grandmother" to Tara, hosted a lavish dinner for her.
>
> Her great grandfather, Bhara Nana, took her to the gurwara, the Sikh temple. We went to a Hindu temple. Tara and Leela prayed, taking it very seriously.
>
> Her grandmother took Tara to an orphanage to give some food and money. A home for 461 girls, Tara was swept off her feet by giggling, happy girls who held her hands and stroked her hair. 100 girls in a classroom sang Happy Birthday to her. Tara shyly beamed feeling so special. Tears rolled down my cheeks.
>
> And yesterday, her Dada and Dadi (grandparents) threw a big birthday bash to celebrate her birthday with even more friends and family. By the end of the birthday celebrations it will literally be 5 cakes to celebrate five….

In the United States, as parents got busier with work and parenting responsibilities, and children became pre-teens and teenagers, for some, parties became more about friends than family. Celebrations moved from the home to outside locations such as restaurants, indoor playground entertainment centers, or movie theatres with children or teens being dropped off by their parents who would then return three or four hours later. But some families have two birthday celebrations: one for family and extended family, perhaps a special dinner out or a favorite home-cooked meal, and another for friends.

John and Christine Barnitz, parents of four children as well as educators, advocate bringing parties for young children back into the home and including storytelling and literature in a party themes. In their article, "Celebrating with language and literature at birthday parties and other childhood events," published in *The Reading Teacher*, they also recommend using books as party favors "as welcome gift alternatives to toys that do not last; stories do last in the minds and hearts of children."

BIRTHDAY CARDS

Birthday cards are so common today that it is hard to imagine a world without these welcome birthday reminders that you remember someone – or are remembered by others. Alas, the tradition of sending a birthday card is said to have begun only100 years ago, in England, as a way of expressing one's regrets that it was not possible to visit in person on someone's birthday.

A survey of 2,000 Americans between the ages of 10 and 69 conducted in 1995 by Yankelovitch Partners and American Greeting Cards found that over 1 billion birthday cards were sold annually and that women reported receiving ten birthday cards; men reported receiving eight.

There are today so many commercial cards to choose from, in all price ranges, serious or funny styles including cards that allow a personalized recording. You can also create a homemade card, completely by hand or aided by the simplest or more complex computer design software.

A change in birthday card options within the last decade is the growth of sending free e-cards (electronic) cards over the Internet, some with music playing as well, although some greeting card companies also offer site visitors the opportunity to customize a card and then to print it out.

If you are extremely busy, if you prefer traditional store bought cards to electronic ones, you might consider buying several cards in advance so you have a card handy for every upcoming birthday over the next few weeks or even months. That could help avoid the last minute scrambling to find a card that can sometimes take the joy out of remembering someone's birthday when you are under the pressure of time.

BIRTHDAY SONGS

Certainly the most famous Happy Birthday song is the simple ditty, 'Happy birthday to you" which was composed in 1893 by two sisters, Patty and Mildred Hill, who were schoolteachers living in Louisville, Kentucky. Its original title was "Good morning to you." In 1935, 11 years before Patty Hill died, the song was copyrighted. In 1989, Warner Communications purchased the "Happy Birthday" song for $22 million dollars. It continues to bring in royalties because every time the song is used in a movie, commercial, or TV show, a licensing fee has to be paid. The copyright on the song has been extended till at least 2030.

There are of course other happy birthday songs sung around the world, in different languages. Two other English language examples, although certainly not as famous as "Happy birthday to you," are Stevie Wonder's "Happy Birthday" 1981 song, that helped launch a national holiday for the late civil rights leader Martin Luther King Jr., and the "Happy Birthday" song by the Beatles.

BIRTHDAY PRESENTS

The American Greetings survey mentioned previously also found that personal items were the most common birthday gifts (83%) with clothing (57%), money (29%), and jewelry (16%) the most popular choices.

Consider the birthday presents you have received over the years. Is there anything memorable that might offer clues about what to get for your loved ones? Better yet, do you get any hints of what someone would need or want?

When exchanging gifts with friends, "it's the thought that counts" tends to be the overall philosophy. You might buy your children or spouse a major ticket item birthday gift, in addition to dining out, whether it's clothes, fine jewelry, or electronic equipment. But for a friend, birthday gifts may be costume jewelry, a book, a DVD of a movie, clothing, or going out to lunch or dinner.

Should you wrap a birthday present? In many countries including India and the United States, the wrapping of a present can be seen as a significant part of gift giving. There is scientific evidence to support the positive impact of a wrapped present: Daniel J. Howard, in the Department of Marketing at Southern Methodist University in Texas, did an experiment to see how gift-wrapping impacted on the study participant's attitude toward a gift. In all four experiments, wrapped presents made the study subjects feel happier about the gift they were receiving.

Making a donation to a charity in the name of the birthday boy or girl is another way to mark a family member or friend's special day, particularly if he/she is having a party and has instructed loved ones: "no presents."

BIRTHDAY CELEBRATIONS AROUND THE WORLD

According to Bebbe Lauritzen, who lives and works in Denmark, "it is a common tradition to fly a flag in honor of a person celebrating a birthday. If you have a flagpole in your garden, the flag will be run up at sunrise (at the earliest at 8 am) whenever you have something to celebrate (birthdays, anniversaries etc.) and the flag will be lowered before sunset. Children are often celebrated with flags in birthday cakes. In school and/or kindergarten, there may be a flag at the seat of the child having his/her birthday. "

Estrella Chan, who now lives in Seattle, Washington and is founder of English Around the World, a company that teaches English as a foreign language to immigrants, grew up in a Chinese family in Hong Kong. Notes Estella: "I don't remember birthday parties as children; only dinners at home in which guests were not told that it was a birthday celebration. Chinese consider it impolite to let people know it's your birthday because that obligates them to buy you a gift. Therefore, there's no birthday song. And if a friend actually knows it's your birthday and brought you a gift, it's polite to wait till after the guest leaves to open the gift."

A children's party activity, which is said to have originated in ancient Mexico, and has spread to other Latin American countries as well as to Europe , the United States, and elsewhere, is the tradition of hitting the *piñata*. A piñata, as most know, is a container made out of clay or paper mache, that is filled with candies or small toys. Party goers may have their eyes blindfolded as they hit the piñata with a stick or a bat or use an alternative "pull string" way of getting at the goodies inside, until the candies or toys fall to the ground and the guests scramble to pick up what falls to the ground.

There is a custom that has become popular in the United States whereby someone will put a life-size cutout figure on the lawn, wishing the birthday girl or boy a happy birthday, and, at the same time, announcing to the world that someone is celebrating a birthday. For more practical reasons, like helping visitors to find the house where they are going for birthday celebration, balloons may be tied around a mailbox or a door knob to indicate the party destination.

It is also important to remember that some religions and cultures do not celebrate birthdays, possibly because of the pagan roots of the custom, among other reasons. So before you throw a surprise party for your friend whose religion is known to ignore birthdays, find out if she/he follows that philosophy and if a party, presents, or even a card would be a welcome tribute.

CERTAIN BIRTHDAYS GET MORE ATTENTION

In each culture, there are certain birthdays that seem to have more importance than others. In the United States, whenever possible, all the birthdays until ten are celebrated in some special way by family, friends, or schoolmates. As children enter their teen years, parties become less frequent and are more likely for turning a certain age, especially 16, 18, and then 21, 25, and each decade from 30 on.

In Korea, on the 100th day after a child's birth, it is the custom to have a celebration to mark that the baby has gotten through these challenging early months of life. There is also a lot of fuss for the first birthday, or the *tol*, celebration since making it to the first year in bygone years when infant mortality was much higher was another milestone.

Nigerians consider the 1st, 5th, 10th, and 15th birthdays special.

In Japan, the 3rd, 5th, and 7th birthdays are considered more significant. Also, September 15th, *Kiero No Hi*, or "Respect for the Aged Day," is celebrated with gifts given to residents who are becoming 70 years of age.

In China, for thousands of years it has been a custom to have a big party when a senior turns sixty or eighty. "Most families will invite relatives, close friends, colleagues, or neighbors for a big dinner party," notes a colleague.

A "golden birthday" happens once; it is when the age on a birthday is the date of the month someone was born in. So if your child was born on April 14th, her golden birthday is fourteen. (Joan Bramsch has been popularizing this concept, something her family has practiced for 50+ years, since 1998.)

Turning 100 is cause for a celebration; in the United States it has become a tradition to see centenarians singled out with their photos by Willard Scott on the NBC morning talk show, the *Today Show.*

CERTAIN BIRTHDAYS GET LESS ATTENTION – BUT THAT SHOULD CHANGE!

IF YOU OR SOMEONE YOU LOVE have a birthday that is during a month when there are other major celebrations, such as December, it is possible your birthday may be minimized (or you may be tempted to include your friend or family member's birthday gift or greetings along with your gift or well wishes for the other occasion). Psychiatrist Susan Delphine Delaney knows, first hand, what that feels like, multiplied by three. As she explains: "The three oldest children in our family were born within two years of one another and all at Christmas-time: December 23rd, December 25th, and January 4th." As a December baby herself, her advice is: "I tell all my patients who have kids with Christmas birthdays to make a big deal of it."

BIRTHDAY REMEMBRANCES

You might want to ask yourself what birthday traditions from your childhood and formative years are most special to you. Those might be the traditions you want to continue, or you and your family, and your friends, might want to create your own unique ways of celebrating.

Based on research published in the *New England Journal of Medicine*, you might want to be somewhat cautious about throwing someone a surprise party. As Dr. W. Gifford Jones writes: "…[if] you're considering taking an old friend surreptitiously out for a quiet dinner. And it's your intention to have them open a door to encounter a room full of people. Think twice if it's an elderly person who has a history of previous heart problem. A sudden flow of adrenaline is the last thing this person needs. In this case the best surprise is no surprise."

Also be sensitive to the powerful meaning a birthday may have for some as a time to reflect. It may also be a time for you and your loved ones to gather to mark the birthday of a deceased loved one, to celebrate his/her life as so many cultures do when marking the birthdays of our past leaders, heroes, and heroines.

Remembering someone's birthday can be through a phone call, a text message or e-mail, a present, a party, or a visit. What matters most is that you make an effort to show those you care about that you recall him/her on their special day, their birthday. If possible, try to have your card or gift arrive on that day or, if necessary, before instead of afterwards. (But it is still better late than never, as the saying goes, which is why they invented "belated birthday cards.") You might also want to call on your dear one's birthday, even if you have to leave a voice or text message because the birthday boy or girl is out celebrating.

Marking your family member, romantic partner, or friends' birthday in some special way is a thoughtful effort on your part that will surely be appreciated. This *Birthday Tracker and Journal* will help you to keep all the information about the birthdays of those you care about in one convenient, central place as well as a journal for writing your birthday reflections.

REFERENCES

Argetsinger, Kathryn. "Birthday Rituals: Friends and Patrons in Roman Poetry and Cult." *Classical Antiquity*, volume 11, October 1992, pages 175-193.

Barnitz, John and Christine Gora Barnitz. "Celebrating with Language and Literature at Birthday Parties and Other Childhood Events." *The Reading Teacher*, October 1996, pages 110-117.

Batt, Linda. "Making the Big Day Special." *Mothering* July-August 2000, page 55.

"Birthdays are bastions of emotion and ritual." *Greetings Magazine*, Feb 1995, p. 12+.

"Birthday Traditions From Around the World," http://www.coolest-kid-birthday-parties.com/birthday-traditions.html

Chopra, Mallika. "A Birthday in India," January 14, 2007, http://www.intentblog.com/archives/2007/01/a_birthday_in_i.html

Gifford-Jones, M.D., W. "Think Twice Before Arranging a Surprise Party." December 8, 2006, http://www.canadafreepress.com/medical/medical-notes120806.htm

"Happy birthday and so long," *Science News*, October 10, 1992, page 237.

"History of Birthday Cake," Tokenz, Lucknow, India, http://www.tokenz.com/history-of-birthday-cake.html

Howard, Daniel J. "Gift-Wrapping Effects opn Product Attitudes: A Mood-Biasing Explanation." *Journal of Consumer Psychology*, volume 1 (1992), pages 197-223.

Kleinman, Kathyrn. *Birthday Cakes: Recipes and Memories from Celebrated Bakers.* San Francisco: Chronicle Books, 2004.

Korab, Holly. "A Brief History of Birthday Parties," U of Illinois, alumni magazine, 2001.

Neville, Lee. "Birthdays everywhere." *Child Life*, July-August 1995, page 28+

Watson, Kristen. "Unwelcome birthday surprise," *Prevention*, October 2006, page 38.

Wax, Emily. "Birthday Bashes That Take the cake." *Washington Post*, July 31, 2007.

How to Use This Birthday Tracker and Journal

I know it is possible today to track the birthdays of your family and friends on a computer through social media sites like Facebook or in your smart phone or cell phone. But you still might find it useful to have a physical central place where all the birthday information is kept, especially if you are tracking birthdays for numerous family members and friends.

Whether you send a card, exchange birthday presents, or just pick up the phone and call your family members, friends, or neighbors to wish them a happy birthday, it will be easier to keep track of all those dates with this handy tracker and journal. In addition to the month-by-month tracker — you put the name of everyone having a birthday on a specific date on that date in the tracker, including a phone number or e-mail address, if you wish, as well. Between each month is a color reproduction of one of my original collages, drawings, or paintings.

In the back of this tracker, you will find a place to record contact information for key family and friends. A month-by-month list of birthstones and flowers follows that might be useful for gift consideration. You will then find a place to record what presents (or cards) you send to someone for his/her birthday, year after year. That might help you to be less likely to send the same kind of gift one or two years later. There is also by a place to track what gifts (or cards) that you receive and when you send (or call) a thank you.

Birthdays are special times, to reflect on our own lives, or on the life of the person whose birthday we are celebrating, so you will find blank lined pages in the back of this tracker/journal where you can record your thoughts. You might even want to use these blank lined pages in the journal part of this tracker to plan your next birthday celebration.

You will also find a place in this tracker and journal to add photos if you want to include birthday-related pictures in this record book.

Happy celebrating! I look forward to your feedback that this illustrated birthday tracker and journal has become one of your treasured family keepsakes. You might also find that this unique *Birthday Tracker and Journal* makes a perfect birthday gift for a family member, friend, or colleague.

I welcome hearing from you about birthday customs that you would like to share with me. Here is my e-mail address: yagerinquiries2@aol.com.

Best Wishes,

Jan Yager

janyager.com

"There was a star danced, and under that was I born."
—WILLIAM SHAKESPEARE

"The more you praise and celebrate your life,
the more there is in life to celebrate."
—OPRAH WINFREY

Birthdays In *January*

1.

2.

3.

4.

5.

6.

7.

January

8.

9.

10.

11.

12.

13.

14.

Birthdays In *January*

15.

16.

17.

18.

19.

20.

21.

January

22.

23.

24.

25.

26.

27.

28.

Birthdays  January

29.

30.

31.

Notes

Birthdays In February

1.

2.

3.

4.

5.

6.

7.

February

8.

9.

10.

11.

12.

13.

14.

Birthdays In February

15.

16.

17.

18.

19.

20.

21.

February

22.

23.

24.

25.

26.

27.

28.

Birthdays  In February

29.

Notes

Birthdays  In March

1.

2.

3.

4.

5.

6.

7.

March

8.

9.

10.

11.

12.

13.

14.

Birthdays In March

15.

16.

17.

18.

19.

20.

21.

March

22.

23.

24.

25.

26.

27.

28.

Birthdays  March

29.

30.

31.

Notes

Birthdays In April

1.

2.

3.

4.

5.

6.

7.

April

8.

9.

10.

11.

12.

13.

14.

Birthdays  April

15.

16.

17.

18.

19.

20.

21.

April

22.

23.

24.

25.

26.

27.

28.

Birthdays  April

29.

30.

Notes

Birthdays  May

1.

2.

3.

4.

5.

6.

7.

May

8.

9.

10.

11.

12.

13.

14.

Birthdays  *May*

15.

16.

17.

18.

19.

20.

21.

May

22.

23.

24.

25.

26.

27.

28.

Birthdays  May

29.

30.

31.

Notes

 Birthdays In June

1.

2.

3.

4.

5.

6.

7.

June

8.

9.

10.

11.

12.

13.

14.

Birthdays  *June*

15.

16.

17.

18.

19.

20.

21.

June

22.

23.

24.

25.

26.

27.

28.

Birthdays  In June

29.

30.

Notes

Birthdays  July

1. _____

2. _____

3. _____

4. _____

5. _____

6. _____

7. _____

July

8.

9.

10.

11.

12.

13.

14.

Birthdays In July

15.

16.

17.

18.

19.

20.

21.

July

22.

23.

24.

25.

26.

27.

28.

Birthdays  July

29.

30.

31.

Notes

Birthdays In August

1. _____

2. _____

3. _____

4. _____

5. _____

6. _____

7. _____

August

8.

9.

10.

11.

12.

13.

14.

Birthdays In August

15.

16.

17.

18.

19.

20.

21.

August

22.

23.

24.

25.

26.

27.

28.

Birthdays  In August

29.

30.

31.

Notes

Birthdays In September

1.

2.

3.

4.

5.

6.

7.

September

8.

9.

10.

11.

12.

13.

14.

Birthdays In September

15.

16.

17.

18.

19.

20.

21.

September

22.

23.

24.

25.

26.

27.

28.

Birthdays  September

29.

30.

Notes

Birthdays *In* October

1.

2.

3.

4.

5.

6.

7.

O_{ctober}

8.

9.

10.

11.

12.

13.

14.

Birthdays  *October*

15.

16.

17.

18.

19.

20.

21.

October

22.

23.

24.

25.

26.

27.

28.

Birthdays  October

29.

30.

31.

Notes

Birthdays  In November

1.

2.

3.

4.

5.

6.

7.

November

8.

9.

10.

11.

12.

13.

14.

 Birthdays In November

15.

16.

17.

18.

19.

20.

21.

November

22.

23.

24.

25.

26.

27.

28.

 Birthdays In November

29. _____

30. _____

_____

Notes

_____

_____

_____

_____

_____

_____

_____

_____

_____

Birthdays  In December

1.

2.

3.

4.

5.

6.

7.

December

8.

9.

10.

11.

12.

13.

14.

Birthdays  In December

15.

16.

17.

18.

19.

20.

21.

December

22.

23.

24.

25.

26.

27.

28.

Birthdays  In December

29.

30.

31.

Notes

CONTACT EMAIL/ADDRESS/PHONE/SOCIAL MEDIA DIRECTORY

NAME

ADDRESS

PHONE

EMAIL

NOTES

NAME

ADDRESS

PHONE

EMAIL

NOTES

NAME

ADDRESS

PHONE

EMAIL

NOTES

NAME

ADDRESS

PHONE

EMAIL

NOTES

Contact Email/Address/Phone/Social Media Directory

NAME

ADDRESS

PHONE

EMAIL

NOTES

NAME

ADDRESS

PHONE

EMAIL

NOTES

NAME

ADDRESS

PHONE

EMAIL

NOTES

NAME

ADDRESS

PHONE

EMAIL

NOTES

Contact Email/Address/Phone/Social Media Directory

NAME

ADDRESS

PHONE

EMAIL

NOTES

NAME

ADDRESS

PHONE

EMAIL

NOTES

NAME

ADDRESS

PHONE

EMAIL

NOTES

NAME

ADDRESS

PHONE

EMAIL

NOTES

BIRTHSTONES

January Garnet

February Amethyst

March Aquamarine

April Diamond

May Emerald

June Pearl, Moonstone

July Ruby

August Peridot, Sardonyx

September Sapphire

October Opal, Tourmaline

November Topaz, Citrine

December Turquoise, Blue Topaz

BIRTHDAY FLOWERS

January — carnation or snowdrop
February — iris
March — daffodil
April — daisy or sweet pea
May — lily of the valley
June — rose
July — larkspur
August — gladiolus or poppy
September — aster or morning glory
October — marigold
November — chrysanthemum
December — poinsettia or narcissus
(daffodil or jonquils)

BIRTHDAY CARD / GIFT RECORD
Sent

NAME	DATE SENT	ITEM (PRESENT/CARD)

BIRTHDAY CARD / GIFT RECORD
Sent

NAME	DATE SENT	ITEM (PRESENT/CARD)

Birthday Card / Gift Record
Sent

Name	Date Sent	Item (Present/Card)

BIRTHDAY CARD / GIFT RECORD
Received

FROM NAME	DATE RECEIVED	ITEM (PRESENT/CARD)	THANK YOU (CALL/NOTE)

BIRTHDAY CARD / GIFT RECORD
Received

FROM NAME	DATE RECEIVED	ITEM (PRESENT/CARD)	THANK YOU (CALL/NOTE)

BIRTHDAY CARD / GIFT RECORD
Received

FROM NAME	DATE RECEIVED	ITEM (PRESENT/CARD)	THANK YOU (CALL/NOTE)

Birthday Notes / Journal Entries

BIRTHDAY NOTES / JOURNAL ENTRIES

BIRTHDAY NOTES / JOURNAL ENTRIES

BIRTHDAY NOTES / JOURNAL ENTRIES

Birthday Notes / Journal Entries

BIRTHDAY NOTES / JOURNAL ENTRIES

Birthday Picture Album

Place
Photo
Here

Place
Photo
Here

Place
Photo
Here

Place
Photo
Here

BirthdayPicture

Album

Place
Photo
Here

Place
Photo
Here

Birthday Celebrations

www.birthdaycelebratations.net

Free site that provides information on the history of the birthday cake, party, and song with short entries on birthday celebration traditions country-by-country around the world including Australia, Brazil, Germany, Denmark, China, Canada, and Vietnam.

Famous Birthdays

www.famousbirthdays.com

Free site that has a search function that takes you to the birthday you want to know about and then lists the name of famous people who have that birthday, plus the year they were born.

Golden birthday

www.goldenbirthdaybook.com

Site by Joan Bramsch around the concept of a golden birthday: when you are the same age as the day of the month you were born on. (Someone born on March 25th would have a golden birthday when she/he turned 25.)

123 Greetings

http://www.123greetings.com/birthday/

Free birthday e-cards.

Hallmark

www.hallmark.com

You can send free e-cards, subscribe to their premium service or buy paper cards from this site.

American Greetings

www.americangreetings.com

Offers free e-cards plus birthday cards that can be printed as well as a free reminder program for birthdays and other holidays that you can sign up for.

Hannacroix Creek Books, Inc.

www.hannacroixcreekbooks.com

Go to the "Journals" section at the publishing company's site. At the entry for this book, you will find additional birthday resources including anecdotes and examples, birthday photographs, as well as a selected list of birthday videos available at youtube.com.

Dr. Jan Yager

www.drjanyager.com

Author/illustrator's main website including free book excerpts, article reprints and the original blog, http://www.drjanyager.com/blog.

About the Author & Artist

Self-portrait

JAN YAGER is a sociologist/speaker/writer/artist
who lives in Fairfield County, Connecticut.

For more information, go to: www.janyager.com

Personal journal

Time to Lose journal

Provides a place to keep track of your daily dieting and exercise efforts as well as space to put your diet plan; includes the 7 principles of creative weight management and a place to list favorite recipes, and to record your notes and thoughts.

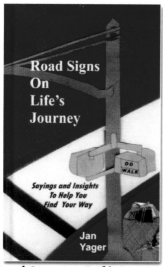

Road Signs on Life's Journey

This collection of 257 original sayings by this sociologist/author and famous quotes is the perfect gift for the graduate or for anyone starting a new venture. Covers friendship, love, reading, joy, studying, family, writing, and lots more.

Friendship journal with select quotes on friendship excerpted from Friendshifts